Note to parents, carers and teachers

Read it yourself is a series of modern stories, favourite characters, traditional tales and first reference books written in a simple way for children who are learning to read. The books can be read independently or as part of a guided reading session.

Each book is carefully structured to include many high-frequency words vital for first reading. The sentences on each page are supported closely by pictures to help with understanding, and to offer lively details to talk about.

The books are graded into four levels that progressively introduce wider vocabulary and longer text as a reader's ability and confidence grows.

Ideas for use

• Begin by looking through the book and talking about the pictures. Has your child heard this story or looked at this subject before?

• Help your child with any words he does not know, either by helping him to sound them out or supplying them yourself.

• Developing readers can be concentrating so hard on the words that they sometimes don't fully grasp the meaning of what they're reading. Answering the quiz questions at the end of the book will help with understanding.

For more information and advice on Read it yourself and book banding, visit www.ladybird.com/readityourself

Book Band 5

Level 1 is ideal for children who have received some initial reading instruction. Stories are told, or subjects are presented very simply, using a small number of frequently repeated words.

Special features:

Opening pages introduce key subject words

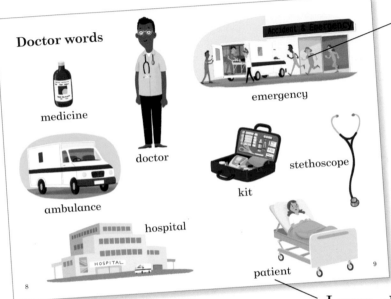

Large, clear labels and captions

Careful match between text and pictures

Educational Consultant: Geraldine Taylor
Book Banding Consultant: Kate Ruttle
Subject Consultant: Dr Vashti Mason

LADYBIRD BOOKS

UK | USA | Canada | Ireland | Australia
India | New Zealand | South Africa

Ladybird Books is part of the Penguin Random House group of companies
whose addresses can be found at global.penguinrandomhouse.com

www.penguin.co.uk www.puffin.co.uk www.ladybird.co.uk

First published 2017
This edition published 2017
001

Printed in China

A CIP catalogue record for this book is available from the British Library

ISBN: 978-0-241-32787-6

All correspondence to
Ladybird Books
Penguin Random House Children's Books
80 Strand, London WC2R 0RL

I am a Doctor

Written by Katie Woolley
Illustrated by John Lund

Contents

Doctor words

medicine

doctor

ambulance

hospital

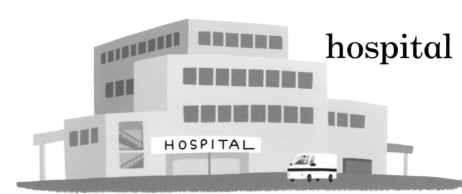

HOSPITAL

emergency

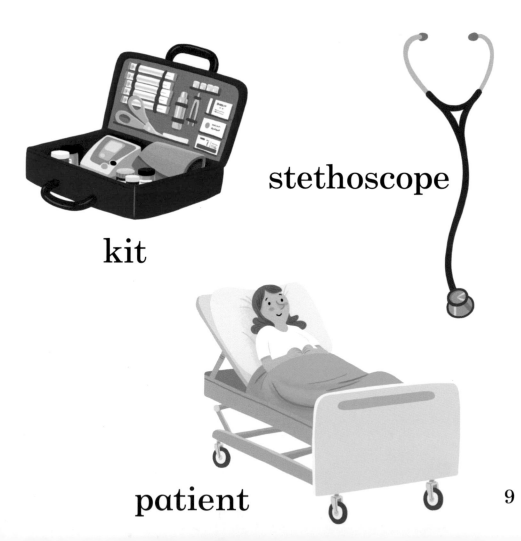

kit

stethoscope

patient

A doctor's day

A doctor helps sick people get better.

Sick people are called patients.

11

At the doctor's surgery

Patients can see the doctor at the doctor's surgery.

Doctor's kit

Doctors have a kit to help patients. The kit has medicine and a stethoscope in it.

I have a stethoscope to help.

kit

medicine

stethoscope

15

In the home

Doctors can go to see some patients at home, too.

The doctor takes a kit with them that helps people get better.

medicine

kit

17

Emergency help

An ambulance takes very sick people to hospital to see a doctor. This is called an emergency.

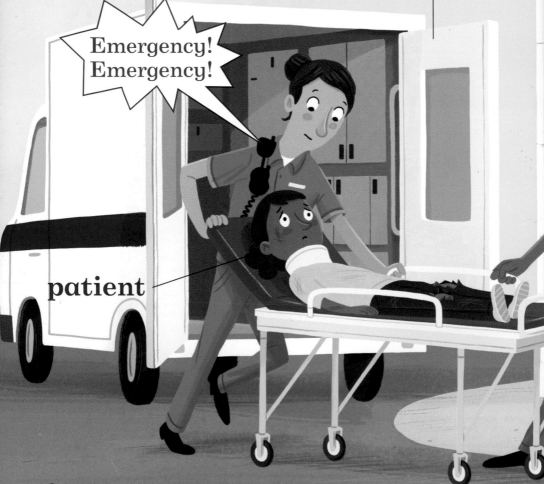

ambulance

patient

18

doctor

19

At the hospital

At the hospital, doctors look after people who are too sick to be at home.

This patient is very sick.

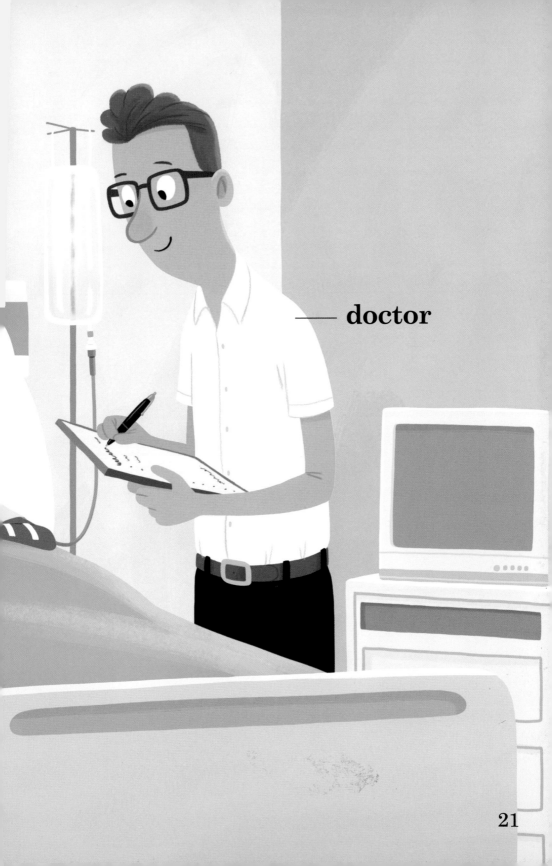

—— **doctor**

21

Stay in hospital

Some patients stay in hospital to get better. A doctor looks after them.

doctor

hospital bed

You are better now. Would you like to go home?

A BIG emergency!

Some doctors go to a big emergency.

I am a doctor and I am here to help.

doctor's kit

They take a doctor's kit
with them to help.

Would you like to be a doctor?

Doctors help patients get better. They have kits and medicine to help people.

They help at the hospital.

They help at a big emergency.

They help at the surgery.

Picture glossary

 ambulance

 doctor

 emergency

 hospital

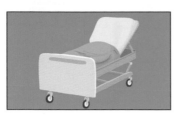 hospital bed

 kit

 medicine

 patient

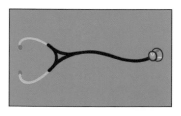 stethoscope

 surgery

Index

I am a Doctor quiz

What have you learnt about doctors?
Answer these questions and find out!

- What are sick people called?

- What do doctors have to help patients?

- Where do very sick people go in an emergency?

Tick the books you've read!

Level 1

☐ ☐ ☐ ☐ ☐

☐ ☐ ☐ ☐ ☐

Level 2

☐ ☐ ☐ ☐ ☐

☐ ☐ ☐ ☐ ☐

Level 3

☐ ☐ ☐ ☐ ☐

Level 4

☐ ☐ ☐ ☐ ☐

  The Read it yourself with Ladybird app is now available